Colonial American Holidays and Entertainment

Colonial American

HOLIDAYS AND ENTERTAINMENT

by Karen Helene Lizon

COLONIAL AMERICA

FRANKLIN WATTS

NEW YORK / CHICAGO / LONDON / TORONTO / SYDNEY

Y
394.26973
LIZ

Photographs copyright ©: Historical Pictures/Stock Montage,
Chicago, IL: pp. 10, 17, 23, 73; The Bettmann Archive: pp. 12, 32, 40,
47, 50, 51, 60, 63, 89, 93, 96; North Wind Picture Archives, Alfred, ME:
pp. 16, 29, 31, 36, 37, 44, 58, 66, 67, 76, 78, 83.

Library of Congress Cataloging-in-Publication Data

Lizon, Karen Helene.
Colonial American holidays and entertainment/by Karen Helene Lizon.
112 p. cm. (Colonial America)
Includes bibliographical references and index.
Summary: Surveys the different holidays celebrated throughout the
year by the early settlers in America and describes some of the
various activities, sports, and toys with which they amused
themselves.
ISBN 0-531-12546-7
1. Holidays—United States—History—Juvenile literature.
2. United States—Social life and customs—Colonial period, ca.
1600–1775—Juvenile literature. [1. Holidays—History.
2. Amusements—History. 3. United States—Social life and customs—
Colonial period, ca. 1600–1775.] I. Title.
GT4803.A2L59 1993
394.2'6973'09032—dc20   92-40262 CIP AC

Contents

Colonial American Holidays and Entertainment

CHAPTER ONE

Early Americans

During the early years of colonization in America, the first settlers worked hard and faced many difficulties. They hoped to create a better way of life for themselves in the colonies.

These colonists came unprepared to face the wilderness, and many of them died from starvation, disease, or in clashes with Native Americans. Their lives were preoccupied with trying to survive, and they were often too tired and sad to think about celebrating holidays and enjoying entertainment.

As more settlers arrived, however, holidays were seen as a time for enjoyment and recreation, and pleasurable activities were looked forward to when possible.

Colonists came from a number of different countries. Some of the early settlers were French, Dutch, English, German, Swedish, Finnish, Polish, Scotch, Irish, African, and Italian.

America's original inhabitants, Native Americans, who had been here for thousands of years, watched as boatloads of newcomers arrived on their shores. These

The early colonists came to America from many
different countries. They were met here by this
country's original inhabitants, Native Americans.

settlers brought along their axes, guns, and diseases, and the Indians soon learned that many of these people came not to share and preserve, but to take and destroy. Their new ways proved hazardous for Native Americans and their culture.

The settlers arrived in the colonies for many reasons. Some hoped to start a business venture that would make them wealthy. Others came searching for the riches they had heard about. Many came seeking a better life for their families than the one they had, and some colonists, like the Puritans and Quakers, came to America looking for religious freedom.

There was a great demand for laborers in the colonies and many settlers came as indentured servants to fill this need. These people were usually poor or working class and faced hard times at home. By signing a contract and agreeing to work for a period of time, usually four to seven years, they could enter the colonies with the hope of one day improving their lives. It is believed that as many as half of the people who came to America during the colonial era came as indentured servants.

Eventually, there weren't enough indentured servants to meet the needs of the plantation owners and farmers. Some colonists turned to slavery as a means of obtaining workers.

The first slaves to arrive in the colonies were brought from the Caribbean, but by the late 1600s slave traders were shipping slaves directly from Africa. The African people were taken from their homeland and didn't enter the colonies of their own free will.

No matter from what country the pioneers came, when they departed from their original homes, they missed many of their traditional folkways, songs, dances, and local celebrations.

They had to face their first holidays struggling in an unfamiliar land without their familiar customs and

traditions. These early Americans had to make the most of their surroundings, and they often found it necessary to adapt traditional ways of observing a holiday or participating in a pastime.

Not until a long time after the colonial era had ended, and our country had begun to expand, did the different cultural traditions of all of the early Americans blend and merge into many of the holiday customs we know today.

Slaves landing at Jamestown, Virginia. The first slaves came from the Caribbean, but later slave traders shipped slaves directly from Africa.

During the winter and spring seasons, the settlers celebrated some of the same holidays we do today and others that are no longer popular.

WINTER DAYS OF CELEBRATION

After a strenuous harvest season, the colonists looked forward to winter's merriment. Even though the daylight hours were short, and the weather often harsh, they found many occasions to have fun.

Imagine rolling out of bed one cold winter morning to find the ponds frozen and school canceled. A holiday, observed in the New York colony (New Netherland), called "First Skating Day," had arrived. The boys and girls, and even the adults, gathered their skates and headed to the ice for the day. This pastime reminded the Dutch settlers of the happy days they had spent skating on the canals in the Netherlands.

As the Christmas season drew near, families began

to get ready for the holiday. Not all of the colonists celebrated Christmas on the same date in December, and some settlers, because of their religious beliefs, did not observe the holiday at all.

The Puritans in New England had a law that didn't permit them to celebrate Christmas and certain other holidays. They did, however, honor three holy days: the Sabbath which they observed faithfully, the Day of Humiliation and Fasting, and the Day of Thanksgiving and Praise. These last two holy days were proclaimed only when the people felt conditions called for it. When times were good, the Puritans believed God was pleased, and they declared a Day of Thanksgiving and Praise. A Day of Humiliation and Fasting was called when events within their community were not going so well.

Jewish families, who had first settled in New Netherland, had their own holy days to observe during the holiday season. They celebrated Hanukkah. A candle was lit on each night of this eight-day festival of lights. These families did not have a temple in which to meet, and their religious services took place in someone's home where all the neighbors would gather.

Native Americans, too, held rituals to honor special days. They believed in giving thanks to the Great Spirit and all of nature's forces such as the sun, rain, and wind. For their celebrations, they often gathered around a huge bonfire to sing songs, dance, and tell stories. Food, prayer, and music were all important parts of their ceremonies. Native Americans were skilled at creating musical instruments from things found in nature. They made drums to beat, rattles to shake, and flutes to blow. They used these instruments at their celebrations.

A variety of holiday customs and beliefs existed throughout the colonies because of the diversity of cultures in early America.

The Germans, who had settled in the Pennsylvania

In colonial America, holidays and special
occasions were celebrated in different
ways by the various groups of people.

Here colonists gather for psalm-singing
in celebration of Christmas.

colony, became known as the Pennsylvania Dutch. The
other colonists had heard the word "Deutsche," meaning German, and confused it with the word "Dutch."
The Pennsylvania Dutch were skilled at many

crafts. During the Christmas season, they took pride in constructing the Christmas crib in detail. They would place straw on the stable floor and arrange animals around the manger.

One group of Germans in Pennsylvania finished their first building on Christmas Eve. They stored their cows in one room and then assembled to sing songs in the adjoining room. They remembered that Jesus had been born in a stable and some of the first sounds he had heard had been from the animals that surrounded him.

An illustration showing Native Americans giving thanks to the Great Spirit

German women were careful not to leave behind their treasured cookie cutters when they started their voyage to their new home. The tasty Christmas treats they made were appreciated by family and friends.

The Swedish settlers in the colony of Delaware had brought their legend of St. Lucia with them and they celebrated St. Lucia's Day on December thirteenth. The Swedes began their Christmas season with a festival of lights. People carrying lighted candles paraded through the town, led by a young girl dressed as St. Lucia. They also told folk stories about Scandinavian gift-bringers who were wee elves that had long beards and wore red caps.

The English settlers in Virginia maintained their Old World traditions of keeping the holiday merry by burning the yule log and entertaining at an "open house." Revelers paraded to all the homes throughout the village on Christmas Eve. They carried a wassail bowl full of spiced ale, sugar, and apples and sang carols of the season.

An early group of English settlers sent to America by Sir Walter Raleigh in the 1500s didn't have much to celebrate. After a terrible winter on Roanoke Island, off the coast of North Carolina, the survivors returned to Britain. Raleigh sent a second group of colonists a short time later under the leadership of John White, who helped the people get settled and then returned to England for supplies. He wasn't able to come back to the colony for over two years. When he did, there was no trace of the settlers. Roanoke became known as the "Lost Colony."

In 1607 the English tried again. This time they settled in Jamestown, Virginia. This became the first permanent English colony in America. The first few years were very hard on the settlers. During the Christmas of 1607, Captain John Smith was taken prisoner by the Powhatan Indians. Smith later claimed his life had been spared when the chief's daughter, Pocahontas, had placed her own head upon his, preventing the Indians from clubbing him to death.

The Christmas of 1608 wasn't much better. The people were sick and hungry. They were on better terms with the Powhatans, and Smith went to ask them for food. He wasn't able to return for the holiday, however, because of bad weather.

During the following winter of 1609, the people faced their gloomiest holiday season ever. This was known as the "starving time," because the remaining colonists were dying in large numbers. By the 1620s, conditions had improved and the people were able to have a festive Christmas.

The Dutch in New Netherland originally celebrated Sinterklaas (Saint Nicholas) Eve and Day on December fifth and sixth. The Dutch women took special pride in baking treats for the holidays. This was an important part of their Christmas tradition. The children knew the Sinterklaas celebration was near when spicy cookies called *speculaas* were prepared.

It was also a Dutch custom to bake a two-foot high cookie in a special mold that resembled St. Nicholas and top it with frosting. This oversized treat was much too large to fit with other sweets into the stockings or wooden shoes of the boys and girls, but they enjoyed it just the same.

On Sinterklass Eve, the young people had fun getting together at one house to paste or wrap a gold or silver leaf on small cakes. This was called *koek-plakken*, or cake-pasting. Dancing, singing, and sharing a meal were all part of the evening's activities.

The children would spread a sheet near the door during the celebration and then wait for the door to burst open. When this happened, a shower of sweets and fruit would drop to the cloth, delighting the youngsters. A man with a long white beard dressed in a bishop's robe and tall hat, and carrying a staff, would enter the home. He would ask the children if they had been good. That night the boys and girls would place their wooden shoes near the fireplace and hope for gifts. They would set out hay, carrots, and water for St. Nicholas's white horse, Sleiper, before going to bed.

The following morning, on Sinterklass Day, good children would find cakes and treats in their shoes, and a child who had been bad might find a switch.

The African slaves enjoyed their Christmas holiday by singing, dancing, and telling stories. Often, restrictions on visiting between plantations were lifted during this time and people could get together to celebrate. Some farmers would create a feast for their slaves. They would serve meals that included meats like hog or sheep, and sweets such as peach cobbler and apple dumplings.

Food played a great part in colonial celebrations, and preparations for the Christmas feast were started weeks in advance. Families hunted for a goose or wild turkey and made the plum pudding and sweet treats before the big day.

Not all families, however, were able to have a lavish dinner, especially during the early years, but most tried to serve a special food or treat in recognition of the occasion.

As they counted down the days until Christmas, the colonists decorated their homes, churches, and villages with ivy, garlands, pinecones, and wreaths. Hanging mistletoe or a "kissing bough" made from evergreen and ribbon in the home was a popular custom.

Some villagers had fun slipping a tiny sprig of mistletoe into party invitations they passed out. This was done to wish their guests good fortune in the coming year.

On Christmas Eve, colonial families gathered to share the festivities with their relatives and friends.

They enjoyed telling stories and singing carols. While everyone was crowded in the parlor, it was fun to play a game of blindman's bluff or to perform a pantomime. Often a musician in the group played the fiddle while everyone danced. During this time, each family tried to practice the familiar customs they had brought from Europe.

Today, children climb into bed on Christmas Eve and dream about Santa Claus and waking to find gifts under the tree. During colonial times, there were no Christmas trees and the children had never heard of Santa. They did, however, await the arrival of other gift-bringers such as Sinterklaas, Father Christmas, Bells-nickle, and Christkindl.

Pleasure was more important to the early settlers than the giving or receiving of gifts. It was not always the custom for children to get a present on Christmas Day.

The English gave tokens of appreciation to servants and craftsmen on the day after Christmas, celebrated in England as Boxing Day.

In the very early years of settlement, a holiday was seen as a time of enjoyment for the grown-ups only. They held parties and everyone sang, danced, and drank. As time went on, however, boys and girls were included in the celebrations and were given Christmas gifts. These were often homemade toys such as a sled or doll, and if their family could afford to keep an animal, a child might get a puppy or pony. The children of wealthy families were given delicate tea sets, fancy dolls, or toy soldiers that had been ordered from Europe and shipped to the colonies on huge boats.

Within the villages, friends who exchanged gifts usually gave something they had made by hand. A pomander was a popular, fragrant gift. It was also customary to give to servants and tradesmen packages filled with food goods.

During the holiday season, the settlers made an extra effort to give to the less fortunate.

Christmas Day was a very religious day for most colonists. They attended church and then joined with their loved ones to share a special Christmas dinner. In the north, families had fun gliding over the snow in their sleighs to reach their holiday destinations.

Trappers, loggers, and some families were isolated in the wilderness. They either had to travel far to spend the day with kinfolk in the village, or celebrate alone. If they couldn't make the long journey to town, they would sometimes gather at the fur trading post to share the day with others living in the wilderness.

Christmas festivities were held in the main meeting room of the post. The room was decorated in bright colors, and the people came dressed in their best clothes. Dinner in the wilderness was much like the feasts being served in the village homes. At the trading post, however, the settlers dined on such things as boiled buffalo hump, beaver tail, smoked buffalo tongue, and dried moose nose.

Native Americans often joined the colonists at the trading post to celebrate. After the meal, everyone danced and enjoyed being in the company of others. Even though all the people didn't speak the same language, they found ways to communicate. It was a pleasant change from their usual lonely days.

As the season of merriment continued, people observed New Year's Eve. Colonists living near the villages waited to hear the church bells ringing at midnight to announce that the New Year had arrived. The ships that were docked in the harbors and the soldiers in their forts fired guns to announce the arrival of the New Year.

New Year's Day was another popular holiday in colonial America. It was customary to hold an open house to receive guests. Neighbors made it a point to visit each other's homes.

A New Year's call in New York in 1640

The Dutch liked to serve drinks such as peach brandy and cherry bounce along with honey cakes and *olijkoecks* (doughnuts) on New Year's Day. When leaving a Dutch home on New Year's Day, guests usually broke off a piece of the "sharing cake" near the front door. This was a way to take home a part of the host's hospitality.

A favorite New Year's recipe served on the southern plantations was "Hoppin' John." This was a dish made of black-eyed peas, pork, and rice.

During the holidays, the plantation owners gave many parties, elaborate balls, and fancy dinners. This gave them a break from the isolation of living on a huge plantation, and the chance to visit with their friends. The English colonists originally gave children a gift on New Year's Day. Many boys and girls started the New Year with a new toy.

A tradition from Europe called "mumming" was carried over into the colonies. Some settlers, dressed in costumes, paraded through the town during the New Year's celebration. They would stop at homes and the townsfolk would try to guess who was hiding behind the masks. This practice usually became wild and was discontinued except in a few places.

It wasn't unusual for the settlers to continue their holiday festivities from Christmas until Twelfth Night (Epiphany) on January sixth.

The Dutch settlers baked a special three-kings-bread for their Twelfth Night festivity. This bread was baked with a bean inside, or, if a family was wealthy, they would place a ring in the bread. The person who got the piece of bread with the bean or ring in it was king for the night. Both children and adults celebrated this holiday. The boys and girls liked to place three candles on the ground, one for each of the kings who visited the baby Jesus, and then dance around the candles. The grown-ups marched from house to house, singing. They were led by three kings, each carrying a lighted star on top of a pole.

The English colonists observed Twelfth Night with wassailing, mumming, parties, and eating a special cake loaded with sugar.

After these two weeks of celebrating were over, the colonists had other days to celebrate during the long winter months. On the second day of February, some colonists celebrated Candlemas Day. This had been a religious festival in their European homeland, but in the colonies it was recognized more as a time for fun. The settlers believed if Candlemas Day appeared bright and clear, winter would linger for a time; but if the day was dark and cloudy, spring would soon arrive.

Our Groundhog Day on February 2 is based on these beliefs. We anxiously wait to see if the furry little creature will predict an early spring.

Valentine's Day was also during the month of February. This holiday was not popular with all of the people, but for those who celebrated it, Valentine's Day served as another chance to brighten the dreary winter. The settlers kept busy making homemade cards decorated with lace, ribbons, and hearts. All the cards—which often included love poems and clever verses—had to be delivered in person.

SPRING DAYS TO HONOR

As the longer, warmer days of spring descended upon the land, the colonists had special days to remember and enjoy.

On the first of April, "April Fools' Day," colonial children had the rare opportunity to play a practical joke on their teacher or some other adult. Life was usually very strict for children, both at school and at home, but on this day, boys and girls took great pleasure in getting away with a few tricks.

Shrovetide was a holiday celebrated on the three days preceding Ash Wednesday. During these days, the Dutch participated in wild and noisy activities.

Easter was not widely observed during colonial times. Some settlers celebrated the day by going to church and then doing their usual chores.

The Dutch settlers, however, did honor the day with a little merriment. They decorated eggs for the holiday by scratching designs such as tulips and butterflies onto the egg's surface. They also colored the eggs with natural dyes made from spinach water, beet juice, onion skins, and tree bark.

Colonial children, unlike boys and girls today, had never heard of an Easter bunny who delivers baskets filled with eggs and goodies.

Some weeks after Easter, the Dutch observed *Pinkster Dagh* (Pentecost). This was a special day for feasting and visiting. On this religious holiday, the Dutch hostess served soft waffles. A flower procession was also part of the celebration. In Holland, people had carried tulips, but in the colonies, they carried the native pink or purple azalea (pinkster). Africans who lived in New Netherland enthusiastically participated in the *Pinkster Dagh* celebration and their traditional dances and music were incorporated into the festivities. The celebration lasted about a week.

Jewish families celebrated Passover during this season. They ate special foods such as matzohs (unleavened bread) and retold ancient stories about Moses leading the Hebrew slaves out of Egypt.

Many early settlers considered May Day, the first day of May, their favorite holiday. In the early morning, the villagers would go out and gather fresh flowers. This was called going "a-maying." They would decorate a pole with ribbon and flowers they had collected. The people would then dance and sing around the Maypole. Some colonists even honored the day by firing their guns.

The Puritans didn't believe in celebrating this holiday. Thomas Morton, who had lived in New England, but wasn't a Puritan, celebrated the first May Day by making a Maypole and dancing around it. This made the Puritans so angry that they sent Morton back to England.

CHAPTER THREE

Summer and Fall Holidays

A s the seasons changed, the settlers remembered familiar holidays. They also found new occasions for rejoicing.

A SUMMER OBSERVANCE

Our most popular national holiday, the Fourth of July, or Independence Day, was not celebrated until the colonial era had almost ended. The Declaration of Independence was drafted and signed in the year 1776. American pioneers wanted their freedom, and they no longer wanted to be ruled by England. On July 4, 1776, the colonies proclaimed America an independent nation.

The first Independence Day was observed in Philadelphia on July 4, 1777. People called the day "the Glorious Fourth" and celebrated with church bells ringing, special ceremonies, bonfires, and a thirteen-gun salute.

Some of the Founding Fathers had been influenced by the way American Indians governed their tribes. Benjamin Franklin was one of the men who had sat and listened to the Iroquois chiefs. He was impressed by what he had heard, and he started to imagine and plan an American nation similar to the Five Nation Confederacy formed by the Onondaga, Cayuga, Seneca, Oneida, and Mohawk tribes of the Iroquois Indians. Franklin realized that if the states joined together, America could be a strong country.

AUTUMN DAYS TO REMEMBER

The colonists had plenty of work to do during the crisp autumn days. They had to bring in the harvest and get ready for the long winter ahead. Despite their busy schedules, the people made time to observe and enjoy special days.

The Jewish settlers honored two holy days during this season—Rosh Hashanah, the Jewish New Year, and Yom Kippur, sometimes called the Day of Atonement. Jewish families remembered the important day of Yom Kippur with fasting and prayer. For Jewish colonists, Yom Kippur was the most sacred day of the year.

In the fall, some people were fearful that evil spirits roamed around the earth at Halloween. They offered sweet treats and dressed in costumes to frighten wicked spirits away.

The Irish settlers carried their tradition of All Hallows' Eve to the colonies with them. These were beliefs that had originated with the ancient Celtic tribes. The Irish colonists also passed along the skill of carving

An October harvest scene in New England

pumpkins into jack-o'-lanterns and the idea of playing pranks.

Some colonial families celebrated Halloween with parties where they played games, went on hayrides, and pulled taffy.

On the fifth of November, some anti-Catholic settlers recognized a holiday called Pope's Day. This event was popular in northern cities like Boston. Crowds of boys and young men paraded through the town carrying dummies that they had dressed like the Pope or Catholic priests. The boys usually divided into two gangs, one from south Boston and the other from north Boston. They would toss their dummies into a huge bonfire at the end of the night.

Most people didn't remember the origin of this holiday which was known as Guy Fawkes Day in England, nor had they ever met a Catholic, but this day gave people a chance to dress in costume and act rowdy. The two gangs of boys from south and north Boston didn't get along well, and often the evening ended with a nasty fight erupting between the gangs. Pope's Day celebrations were very rough. Eventually, this unusual holiday lost its appeal and people no longer participated in it.

After the colonists had gathered in their harvest, they observed the ancient tradition of Harvest Home. This was a joyful celebration to recognize a good supply of crops and was celebrated by many people around the world.

At this time of the year, Native Americans also honored their harvest. They held a ceremony to offer prayers and thanksgiving for what they had received. They believed in showing great respect for the earth and all of nature.

Our Thanksgiving holiday is a combination of several past traditions. We remember the Pilgrims who had lived in Plymouth; the joyous feast of celebrating a good harvest; and a religious observance to give thanks to God for a plentiful supply of food.

What we call the first Thanksgiving took place in 1621. The Pilgrims in the Plymouth colony celebrated in their familiar Harvest Home tradition. They feasted,

Native Americans were busy during the fall months, too. Game is dried and smoked for use during the winter.

In 1621, the Pilgrims living in the Plymouth colony held a Thanksgiving celebration with some of the local native people.

held competitions, and played games with the Native Americans for three days. They did not consider this a holy day. If they had, they wouldn't have permitted such festivities.

From time to time, throughout the colonial years,

Thanksgiving feasts were celebrated, but this was not done regularly. When families did observe Thanksgiving, they would gather with their loved ones. This was a special time to visit, feast on good food, and give thanks.

On Thanksgiving, colonial children liked to make corncob dolls, a skill they had learned from the Native Americans, or puppets from vegetables and fruit. After dinner, the boys and girls headed outside to play games in the brisk fall air.

The first national Thanksgiving was established by the Continental Congress in 1777. This day was a time to be solemn and give thanks and not a day to be festive. It wasn't until 1863, during the Civil War period, that President Lincoln announced the first familiar Thanksgiving proclamation. From that time on, one Thursday every autumn was declared a national Thanksgiving Day until it developed into our Thanksgiving celebration of today.

Not all people believe that the Pilgrim's Thanksgiving feast was the first in the New World. Some scholars believe that the first Thanksgiving was celebrated in 1513 when Juan Ponce de Leon landed on Florida's coast and claimed the land for Spain.

It was customary during the sixteenth century for the Spanish explorers to offer thanks to God when they discovered a new shore. In August 1565, a group of Spanish settlers founded St. Augustine, Florida. It is recorded that the explorers sang hymns of thanks, celebrated mass, and feasted with the local people on food from the Spanish ships.

A little more than fifty years later, in 1619, the English who had settled at Berkley Hundred Plantation in Virginia kept the day holy by giving thanks to God and attending a religious service.

These very early Thanksgiving ceremonies didn't include the folk ideas we associate with the holiday such as pumpkin pie, a big turkey, and the Pilgrims. A Thanksgiving was not only held to honor the harvest, but to recognize a safe arrival at a destination or the survival of a harsh winter.

Our Thanksgiving holiday is seen differently by some of the descendants of America's original inhabitants. A group of Wampanoags and other Native Americans join together each year for a ceremony on Thanksgiving Day at Plymouth Rock. They proclaim this a National Day of Mourning. Although the Pilgrims got along well with the Native Americans, future settlers did not. The conflicts that occurred between the Native Americans and the early settlers deprived the native people of their land and much of their culture.

CHAPTER FOUR

Sports and Recreation

Even though the colonists faced many hardships, they found a variety of activities to brighten up their lives. Recreation served a number of useful purposes. Participating in a sport relieved stress, and refreshed the mind and body. Sports also gave the early settlers a chance to get together for fun.

MAKING THE MOST OF NATURE

The very first settlers to arrive in the colonies were not prepared to handle life in the wilderness. Nature had filled the land with a plentiful supply of food, but still many people starved.

Native Americans shared their know-how with the colonists and helped them to adapt to their new surroundings. The Native Americans taught the settlers how to cultivate and grow corn, sweet potatoes, squash, pumpkins, and other vegetables. They showed the

In colonial America, children helped with chores both indoors and outside. Young girls primarily assisted in the home, while boys and girls both searched for nuts, berries, and fruit.

pioneers which wild berries and plants were safe to eat and how to tap a maple tree for sap and boil it down into syrup. They also passed along their tradition of making a clambake. Without their assistance, many more early settlers would have perished.

If the colonists didn't already know how to hunt, trap, and fish for their food upon arriving in the colonies, they had to learn. The woods, skies, lakes, and ocean were filled with many edible foods to keep the people well fed. For holiday feasts especially, families appreciated and took advantage of what nature had provided. A turkey, goose, or pumpkin pie became part of the holiday dinner tradition for many settlers. Drinks like raspberry flummery, made from juicy berries, and whipped syllabub, made with fruit, were served at fancy dinners and holiday parties.

Colonial boys and girls had to pitch in and help provide for their families. Girls assisted mainly in the home, taking care of such tasks as sewing and cooking, while the boys' skills were put to use outdoors.

Young boys were taught how to handle a gun, use a small boat, and sometimes ride a horse. Going off for a few hours of hunting or fishing offered the boys a little freedom away from the watchful eyes at home. A boy felt proud when he returned with a good catch for his family's dinner. Imaginative youngsters considered these outings an adventure.

Colonial children gladly accepted the job of gathering wild berries. They would search through the woods for their favorite kinds. The Native Americans had taught the boys and girls how to locate berries by following the tracks of bears, because these huge animals liked to gobble the fruit off the branches. After a child had collected a big batch of berries, it was given to mother. She would use the fruit to make pies, jellies, jams, and sweet drinks for her family.

Young men liked the challenge of capturing the

wild horses that roamed the untamed land. Hare hunts and fox hunts were also popular activities. The gentry in the south preferred hunting for a fox with hounds. They called this "riding to the hounds" as they had in England. Many northerners, however, preferred hunting for "vermin" like raccoons and opossums.

Men also enjoyed showing off their skills with a rifle at shooting matches where they would aim and shoot at a mark. The lucky winners collected prize money and ribbons.

Many of the male slaves liked to hunt and fish when given the opportunity. In most areas, the law required that a master get permission from the county officials before one of his slaves could carry a gun. Hunting and fishing not only provided the men with a few hours of pleasure, but often yielded a tasty meal as well.

The Puritans participated in many of the outdoor activities such as hunting and fishing, but not on the Sabbath. In many of the colonies, recreation was not permitted on Sundays, but people didn't always obey this law.

ACTIVITIES TO PLEASE

The pioneers preserved many of the enjoyable traditions of their homelands. Other pastimes were invented in the colonies, and some were learned from the Native Americans.

Often the settlers spent a carefree afternoon playing ninepins, shovelboard, skittle, billiards, or bowling on the green. Sometimes indoor games were played in the tavern. Lucky families had a billiard table in their home, and every village had a large grassy square called a green where people could roll a wooden ball. The townsfolk eventually built alleys for the purpose of bowling.

In colonial America the game of "bowls" was played by rolling balls to hit a mark. No pins were used as in modern bowling. Bowling with pins was called ninepins during the seventeenth century. Skittle, which the Dutch called *kégelspel*, was played on a bowling green with a large wooden ball and ninepins. This is the game played by the funny little men described by Washington Irving in his book *Rip Van Winkle*. Shovelboard was a game much like shuffleboard, but instead of being played on a concrete court or on the deck of a cruise ship, shovelboard was played on long tables. Colonial boys created many types of ball games. If they were outdoors, the youngsters most likely kept a game going. They played ball and bat (which was not the same as today's baseball), cricket, wicket, and stool-ball. Stool-ball was played by rolling a ball at a three-legged stool called a cricket while a batter tried to defend it.

Colonial women often got fresh air and exercise by spending an afternoon playing a game of stool-ball.

The English settlers enjoyed balloon ball, a sport that had been popular in England. In this game, players moved quickly over a large field while driving an oversized leather ball back and forth.

Pitching quoits, which is similar to pitching horseshoes, delighted many settlers. In quoits, a player tossed rings at a stake.

Tennis and battledores were also favorite games.

The game "bowls" and the game "skittle" (which the Dutch called *kégelspel*) were two very popular pastimes in colonial America.

Battledores was played by hitting a shuttlecock (birdie) back and forth with a flat wooden paddle. Among the well-to-do, fencing and jousting were enjoyed. Sabers and lances were the weapons of choice in these sporting events of skill and danger. Jousting was done on horseback, and opponents tried to knock each other off with their lances.

Among all the colonists, running was a popular form of recreation. People loved to compete with each other and held races to determine who was the fastest runner.

On hot sunny days, people looked forward to swimming and boating. Swimming was a great way for the settlers to cool off after a hard day's work. The colonists also liked to relax aboard a boat and enjoy the water and bask in the warm sunshine. Swimming contests and canoe races were also popular activities.

In Virginia, people enjoyed Colonial Sports Day when they played games and held bag and foot races. Some of the young men would perform feats of strength or try to climb a greased pole for a bag of silver that had been placed at the top.

For the slaves, leisure time was especially important. These hours were less supervised than working hours and helped them release their stress with activities like running and wrestling. They also liked to hold competitions to see who was the best athlete.

COLD WEATHER SPECIALTIES

Winter was the season for pleasure. In the north, the cold temperatures and snowy conditions created a winter playground.

The children didn't have far to look for a good time once the snow fell. They threw snowballs and built snow forts, but their favorite winter adventure was sledding. Almost all children, from the youngest to the oldest, owned a sled. They would find a hill and drag their homemade sleds up to the top.

Colonial children, who loved any opportunity to compete with one another, held sliding contests down snow-covered hills. Each slider tried to touch the heels of his feet to the slider in front of him. This was called "going-one-up." Each child hoped to keep moving forward until he was the new leader of the team.

Skating on the frozen rivers and ponds was enjoyed by children and grown-ups alike. The blades of the early skates were made of wood, iron, or even beef bones. The blades were strapped to the boots of the skater.

Skating wasn't the only skill performed on the ice. Curling, kolf, and ice boat races were all favorite pastimes. Kolf and curling were similar to ice hockey. Kolf, which was a favorite Dutch sport, was played with sticks and a hard leather ball. Curling was brought to the new land by the Scottish settlers. The sweepers (players) in this game held brooms and tried to slide a curling rock, made from wood, across the ice into a circle or bull's eye.

Knocking on the cobbler's door and wounded soldier were two of the games where youngsters could prove their abilities at sliding on the ice. In knocking on the cobbler's door, a child would slide across the ice on one foot while stamping repeatedly on the ice with the other foot. A skater knelt on one knee and tried to slide as far as possible while playing wounded soldier.

Native Americans introduced the settlers to snowshoes. These shoes not only helped people trudge across the snow-covered land but also provided a pleasurable form of recreation. People liked this activity and eventually formed snowshoe clubs.

Once horses became common, the northern settlers found sleighing a pleasant pastime. They had fun racing their sleighs through the winter landscape.

ROUGH AND TUMBLE

Participating in certain activities assured the players of a vigorous workout. Football contests were usually played in the late fall. Young male colonists would find a pig's bladder and stuff it with something so that they could kick it around. There were no rules for this game and any number of people could play at once.

Native Americans enjoyed a sport similar to football. They played in their bare feet on a sandy shore where there were no stones. One form of this game was played by men, women, and children, and during this version, there could be no fighting or knocking an opponent down. The object was to make a goal.

The Powhatan Indians in Virginia played a game similar to field hockey. The English called this game bandy. Using a crooked stick, players tried to get a leather ball between two trees.

Some anthropologists believe the southeastern Native Americans copied this game from a similar one played by the Native Americans of the northeast. These Native Americans had been playing this lacrosse-type game long before the white man appeared in the colonies. The game consisted of two teams. The players used sticks to try and hit a ball into the other team's

The favorite winter activity of colonial American children was sledding.

goal. It was a very rough sport and often one village played against another. It wasn't uncommon for each team to consist of a hundred or more players. The Iroquois Indians considered lacrosse a spiritual game. It was a game of the Creator, and held as much importance in their lives during the colonial period as it does today.

PLACE YOUR BETS

Spectator events enticed the settlers into choosing a winner and placing a wager. Wrestling, bullbaiting, cockfighting, and horse racing were betting sports for the colonists.

Each man wanted to prove that he was the strongest during a wrestling match. Native Americans also wrestled against each other to prove their strength.

Horse racing spread to all of the colonies and was enjoyed in early America as it is today. Adults, children, servants, masters, townsfolk, and country folk all loved the horses, and everyone bet on the races. Wealthy settlers, however, were the only people who could afford to breed the animals for sport.

The quarter horse was a special type of horse used in races in the Virginia colony. This animal was bred to run a short distance, a quarter of a mile, in a straight line. Other horses were bred to go longer distances.

Cockfighting and bullbaiting were cruel sports. In spite of this, many people went to see these events and placed bets on them.

Cocks (roosters) were trained to kill. They were equipped with steel spurs to speed the process. People often placed large sums of money on this savage activity, and it wasn't unusual for spectators to make accusations that the fights were unfair. Frequently, trouble broke out in the crowd.

A ball game similar to today's game of lacrosse was
played by Native Americans long before
white people appeared in the colonies.

Bullbaiting usually took place in the outdoor area
of a tavern. In this brutal sport, a bull was chained to a
stake. Four to six dogs were then released, one at a
time, into the area where the bull was chained, until
each dog had been killed by the larger, angry animal.

CHAPTER FIVE

Games and Toys

During the colonial era, families didn't own television sets or video games, and the children weren't able to run to a nearby store and pick up the latest toy. Even though the settlers didn't have instant entertainment like VCRs and Nintendo®, they did have a variety of games to keep them busy.

JUST FOR FUN

Colonial children worked hard. Their families depended on their help. When they did have time away from their chores, however, these boys and girls put their imaginations and skills to good use and made the most of their play time.

Almost every boy owned a jackknife that he used for making many of his own playthings. Toys such as whistles from willow tree branches, windmills, water wheels, and box traps were all popular. Boys also enjoyed playing with toy weapons like pop guns, slings, clubs, or bows and arrows. Native American boys also found it fun to invent clever games using their bows and arrows.

The hoop was a cherished colonial toy that provided hours of pleasure. Wooden hoops were the fastest, and occasionally, a father would make one for his youngster as a gift. If a child wasn't lucky enough to own a wooden one, stripping an iron hoop off an old barrel would do.

Rolling hoops across the land thrilled the children. They discovered the best way to keep a hoop going was by tapping it with a wooden or iron stick with a hooked tip called a crook. Youngsters had fun trying to keep up with their hoops as the hoops went faster and faster. The real challenge came once the hoop started to move downhill. Children had to be quick, or risk losing their toys.

Racing hoops over a flat stretch of ground or on a course with sharp turns tested the children's speed and dexterity. It was considered a great accomplishment to be the child who could keep the most hoops going at once. Some talented youngsters were able to handle three or more.

Native Americans were also skilled with the hoop. They found it an exciting challenge to hurl a spear through one while it was rolling.

If children weren't busy with hoops, they might play with loose pieces of rope they had been lucky enough to find. Skipping to a familiar rhyme like "Teddy Bear," "Eaper Weeper," or "Up a Ladder" kept many youngsters occupied. In the early days, unlike today, jumping rope was usually a pastime enjoyed by boys rather than girls.

Colonial children were delighted to own a top or marbles. Youngsters learned that the trick to keeping a top spinning longer was to stroke it with a whip. Chipstones, peg-in-the-ring, and whip-and-top were a few of the games played with a top.

BOYS AT PLAY.

HERE are three boys at play. Each boy has a hoop, which he strikes with a stick, and it rolls along. It is very pleasant to roll a hoop. If you strike it hard, it flies along very fast, and you must run with all your might to catch it.

You must take care not to drive your hoop among horses. I once knew a little boy playing with his hoop in a street. A horse was coming along, but the boy was looking at his hoop, and he did not see the horse. His hoop rolled close to the horse's fore feet, and the boy ran after it.

The horse was going fast, and he struck the boy with his foot. The boy fell down, and the horse stepped on his leg. The poor boy's leg was broken, and it was many weeks before he got well.

Rolling hoops brought hours
of fun to boys and girls.

Marbles thrilled pioneer youngsters just as they thrill today's children. Ringers was a common marble game in early America. The players drew a large circle and then placed their marbles inside it. The object of this game was to shoot your opponent's marbles out of the ring.

Native Americans had invented marble games long before the Europeans had arrived in the colonies.

Boys liked taking part in a game called skying a copper where they would toss a coin into the air. Another interesting pastime was pitching pennies, called "huzzlecap" by the colonists.

All youngsters loved playing with marbles.
This is a street scene in Richmond, Virginia.

Some children preferred to play jackstones. Small metal pieces called jacks or pebbles were used for this game.

From time to time, when a father wasn't too busy with his own chores, he would work with one of his sons to create wooden toys for the family. They would make wheelbarrows, sleds, carts, blocks, and animals. It was common for boys and girls to own playthings their fathers had made by hand. A hobby horse was a favorite toy of the time. Some little girls were lucky enough to get a cradle or a doll's house equipped with tiny furniture. These homemade toys often lasted through childhood, and it wasn't uncommon for them to be passed along to the next generation in the family.

Some of the other toys colonial children owned included drums, kites, sailboats, balls, looking glasses, scales, masks, and swings. A little colonial girl could pretend to be the mama when she played with her doll. Dolls were usually homemade and often called puppets or babies. Building a tepee and imitating the Indians kept many of the young boys amused.

Children also spent their playtime creating cornhusk dolls during the harvest; cutting out paper dolls with scissors; drawing on a slate; or starting a collection of rocks or birds' eggs.

THEN AND NOW

Many games have stood the test of time. They have been passed down from one generation to the next. Boys and girls today play some of the same games, or variations of those games, that children of long ago played.

The feeling of freedom that comes from being out in the fresh air has always encouraged children to run, jump, and shout.

Tag games were especially popular with colonial youngsters. These games were easy to organize; almost any child could play; and they didn't require any special equipment.

Someone was chosen as "it," often by a counting-out rhyme like "Intry, Mintry, Cutry, Corn," and the game was underway in a short time. Squat tag, thread the needle, I spy, stone poison, How many miles to Babylon?, and turn cap were just a few of the tag games colonial children enjoyed. A favorite in the winter was fox and geese because it was easy to mark out the needed shape of a large wagon wheel in the snow.

Activities like hide-and-seek, blindman's buff, leapfrog, and hopscotch existed in early America as they do now. Hopscotch was usually called "scotch hoppers" and was very similar to today's version. An early English game called hot cockles was much like blindman's buff. In this form of the game, the blindfolded player tried to guess who had tapped him on the back.

On holidays, special occasions, or when nasty weather kept the settlers inside, the kitchen, and later the parlor, became a playroom. On indoor play days, games like bag and stick, snap apple, honey pots, and kitty in the corner kept the youngsters busy.

Snap apple was a particularly daring activity. A player would try to bite into an apple that had been fastened at one end of a stick. The stick had a lighted candle at the other end and was suspended from the ceiling by a string.

Ancient ballads which had been passed down for many years through word of mouth were memorized by the children. Girls and boys recited these ballads and performed pantomimes to the words. Some favorite colonial rhymes were: "Ring Around the Rosy," "London Bridge," "Here We Go Round the Mulberry Bush," "Quaker, Quaker, How Art Thee?," "Here I Brew, Here I Bake, Here I Make My Wedding Cake," "When I Was a Shoemaker," and "Kings and I."

Another beloved pastime was cat's cradle. This well-known skill has been passed down through numerous generations and among many cultures. When a pioneer child found a piece of string and a friend, he or she could perform this activity. Once the ends of the string were tied together, the children looped it around their fingers, creating clever shapes like a cradle, a cross, or a spiderweb.

PLAN YOUR MOVE

Certain games required not only skill but concentration and a little luck as well.

Colonial children often found it necessary to play many of their games using kernels of corn as playing pieces. This meant that the harvest season was a busy and fun time of the year. Checkers, called "draughts," was played this way by the first settlers.

Other board games favored during that time were morelles, also known as "nine men's morris," backgammon, and chess. Backgammon was originally called "tables" because two tables were hinged together in order to play the game.

Dutch colonists liked the challenge of a complicated form of backgammon called tick-tack.

Other games such as dominoes, dice, and cards furnished hours of entertainment for many of the settlers.

Cards had been on board the first boats that brought the colonists to their new homes. Playing cards was forbidden in most areas, but that didn't stop people from playing and gambling with them. Both men and women bet at cards. Maw, honor, ruff, and primero were popular card games of the time.

Playing with dice, called "paw-paw," was a common diversion, and hazard was a favorite dice game. Dice were played everywhere, including in the streets where many boys played. Children were often given money to gamble at dice and a few other amusements.

The country folk weren't left out of these activities. They planned outings to town so they could participate in card and dice games. Even the indentured servants were given a day off for recreation, and they too joined in the playing and gambling. When the slaves had free time, they also amused themselves with cards and dice. Native Americans played similar betting games. The Iroquois in the northeast played a dice game with cherry stones, and the Powhatans in the southeast bet on a game played with reeds that was similar to primero, the English card game. Native Americans often bet their hatchets, bows, arrows, and leather coats in games that lasted for days.

CHAPTER SIX

Social Amusements

Leaving behind loved ones and a familiar culture to settle in a new territory created feelings of isolation and sadness for many of the settlers. The people found life more agreeable if they met with one another to socialize. Most colonists led quiet lives and spent a good deal of their time at home, but on certain occasions, they got together with their neighbors.

FRIENDLY GATHERINGS

Keeping in touch with friends made dull colonial days more pleasant. The colonists valued their friendships and considered a friend a great treasure.

Calling on fellow colonists and having them return the visit offered relief from a lonely existence. Many settlers developed visiting routines. Some people called on their friends on the same day each week. It was common to leave a "calling card" when visiting so that the host or hostess could keep a record of who had stopped by.

Among the plantation owners, visiting took on an even more important role. Plantations were spaced far apart, making it difficult for neighbors to get together. To overcome this problem, it was customary for plantation families to visit back and forth for a few weeks at a time.

On Sunday afternoons when the slaves had a break in their work week, they too had the opportunity to spend time visiting with one another.

Native Americans also believed friendship was a thing of great value. It was a compliment to be called a friend or comrade by Native Americans. This name held special meaning for them, and they didn't bestow it upon someone lightly. Within the tribe, a friend became a constant companion. Friendships were likely to develop in childhood and remain strong throughout life.

When strangers stopped to visit certain Native American groups, they were met outside of the village by several important members of the tribe. These people brought along mats and invited their guests to sit down with them and pass the pipe. After this ceremony, the strangers were invited to enter the village with the Native Americans.

Colonial women in towns found tea parties the perfect reason to meet with the other womenfolk to gossip or discuss topics of interest. The ladies also had the opportunity to show off their favorite baked goods at these teas.

Pioneer families enjoyed planning picnics with neighboring families. People, however, could rarely afford to take off a few hours for leisure, so they combined certain chores with their picnicking. The settlers often gathered berries or fished while they were out.

It's no surprise that the early settlers were eager to attend a fair. These gatherings reminded them of the ones they had gone to in their original homelands. Fairs

Socializing with friends and neighbors
helped ease the loneliness of settling
a new land. This picture depicts an
outdoor tea party in New England.

were held in almost every colony. They usually occurred once or twice a year, often in the spring and fall. The Dutch settlers looked forward to the fair they called "Kermis" each fall.

Colonial fairs lasted from three to ten days. Many activities took place during those days. It was a time for both business and pleasure. People gathered for the purpose of trading, buying, selling, and also having fun.

The settlers had a chance to see a variety of shows while at a fair. Performers worked with puppets, polar bears, and camels to entertain the audience. Fortune-tellers, tightrope walkers, jugglers, and fiddlers were also common sights. People could go bowling; join the boat races; ride the merry-go-round; play a game; or just walk around and look at the animals if they cared to. Contests of all types took place at a fair. People participated in whistling, grinning, singing, and wrestling competitions. Some daring colonists might attempt to catch a goose that was running at full speed, or a pig with a greased tail.

Many of the activities that Americans enjoy today at their state and county fairs are traditions that have been passed down from the early colonial days.

FOR THE PEOPLE

Any occasion where the settlers came in contact with one another gave them the opportunity to socialize. In the villages, stores often served as favorite gathering spots, while families in a country settlement met at the fort. People exchanged ideas and gossiped when they stopped by these places.

Town meetings attracted most of the people within the community for more than political reasons. During the early years of settlement, especially, these discus-

Town meetings offered some citizens
an opportunity to come together,
discuss business, and socialize.

sions provided one of the few chances for people to
come together.

Community meetings were usually held once a year
to decide the town's business. Religious groups also
got together to determine the needs of their congre-
gations.

A favorite form of entertainment for all of the colonists was the court days. All classes of people attended the trials of their fellow colonists. Punishment for a crime most often took place in public. The colonists didn't find it odd that criminals were publicly humiliated.

Planters in the south considered the two "Public Times" held in Williamsburg every year a true delight. On these days, farmers attended meetings of the *General Court* and conducted business with one another. They also went to fairs, fancy parties, plays, and horse races while in the city.

Election Days, or, as the Puritans called them, " 'Lection Days," provided much joy. The people voted in the public square or in an open field. In Boston, the citizens voted on the Common. This was a parcel of land that belonged to and was used by all the members of the community. In the very early years, people cast their ballots using kernels of corn.

On Election Days, the governor was escorted into town with a parade. People listened to speeches, arguments, and debates. There were booths where tasty treats could be purchased.

In New England, African slaves took a holiday at this time. They elected their own "governor" and "king" as a way of mocking the election process of the white society. They took the opportunity to dress in fancy clothes, hold parades, and have their own "inaugural parties" to celebrate their "elections." It was a common practice for the people they had voted for to become important members within the slave community.

Two other occasions that the colonists marked with festivities were Training Days and Commencement Day. On Training Days, all young men of military age were required to attend musters. Each township usually held six training days a year. For the Puritans, this was a rare chance to celebrate. On these days, the men would march to the beat of a drum, ride horses, and shoot at targets, along with other military drills.

In the northern port towns, people called these days "frolics." They combined plenty of recreation and pleasure with their work. In Boston, the training took place on the common. The people took part in foot races and shooting at a mark. They also liked to drink beer as they celebrated.

Commencement Day in Cambridge, Massachusetts, attracted the gentry, who flocked to the city in their coaches. This was the day when boys graduated from Harvard University. (Girls did not attend college then.) The school was opened in the 1600s and was the first college in America. It wasn't originally called Harvard, but two years after it opened, it was given the name by which it is known today.

The rich colonists in Boston and the wealthy parents of the students came to see the boys receive their degrees. Commencement was usually held on a Wednesday, and the festivities lasted four or five days. At this time, people had banquets and parades, played games, sang songs, and greeted friends. They made bonfires and shot off fireworks after dark to celebrate the occasion.

Market day also provided a break from the busy work routines of the colonists. Saturday was market day, and the church bells were sounded to call everyone to the field where the market was being held. The townspeople, farmers, and visiting Indians crowded onto the field to do business with each other.

One place where everyone assembled was church. Most early colonists were very religious and the church was a strong influence in their lives. Some of the people had come to the colonies so they could practice their religious beliefs freely, and in many areas, church attendance was required by law. The people believed that

Another place where everyone assembled
was church. After services,
the colonists got together to chat
and exchange the latest news.

the Lord's Day should be set aside for going to church
and reading the Bible. Many activities were forbidden
on this day.

The Puritans held their services in the meetinghouse. They believed church meant the people, not the
building. The meetinghouse wasn't considered sacred

and was used for other purposes when there wasn't a service.

In the Plymouth colony, Puritans held church services twice a week: once on the Sabbath and then again on Thursday for a lecture. On Sundays, these services took place from nine in the morning until noon and then again from two until five in the afternoon. During the noon intermission on the Sabbath, the churchgoers gathered at a neighboring home, tavern, or "noon-house," also called "Sabba-day-house." In the winter, these places offered the freezing church members a chance to warm up and have a meal before returning for the afternoon sermon.

Inside the meetinghouse, people sat according to their position in society. Wealthy people, dignitaries, and the elderly sat in front pews. Men and women were separated as were boys and girls. If people sat in seats that had not been assigned to them, they would have to pay a fee.

In colonial America people were called to church by the beat of a drum, the ringing of a bell, or the blowing of a horn.

Going to church was the main opportunity for many settlers to socialize with their neighbors. Attending a service was an important event in the lives of most families.

After a sermon, the congregation had the chance to gather in front of the church to greet one another and exchange the latest news about births, marriages, and deaths. It was common practice for a crowd to stroll around the church grounds. This gave the villagers the opportunity to extend dinner invitations, exchange news, and gossip. The settlers like to share a meal with one another after the service.

Young men looked forward to Sundays because after the sermon had ended, they had the opportunity to "see home" their favorite girl. During the trip home, the young couple had a chance to talk and spend some time together.

Itinerant ministers traveled throughout the colonies to preach about God. People considered the arrival of a preacher a great event. Preachers held services in village greens, campsites, forest clearings, and city streets. The settlers prayed, sang songs, clapped hands, shouted, wept, and even fainted at these gatherings. The biggest revival to sweep through the colonies was called the Great Awakening. It occurred during the 1700s and lasted about ten years.

The European colonists hoped to convert the African slaves to Christianity. Since there were many similarities between European and African religious beliefs, many slaves were able to continue their own sacred ceremonies as part of the Christian rituals. Africans also believed in an all-powerful Creator, prayer, and singing.

Native Americans incorporated dance and music into their ceremonies of worship. A shaman, who possessed supernatural powers, performed their rituals. Indians believed that spirituality was a way of life.

The influence of the church lessened as time went on and people found other ways to socialize.

EAT, DRINK, AND CHAT

Colonial taverns and inns gave people a chance to gather with others to share a meal or a few drinks while discussing the latest happenings or topics of mutual interest. They performed an important social service during this period.

Inns and taverns came about for two reasons. First, the tavern, often called an "ordinary" because it served an ordinary meal in the old tradition, provided a place for the people in the community to find food, drink,

Native Americans often incorporated
dance and music into their ceremonies
of worship. Two men sacrifice
tobacco to appease the spirit of the wave.

and entertainment. The second reason was that once
people traveled less frequently by waterways and more
by land, they needed a place to sleep, eat a meal, and
tend to their horses.

Inns were simple places. They usually had a room
for the village barber who was often the dentist as well.
Imagine getting your hair trimmed and teeth pulled at
the same time!

Once a tavern or inn was built, it became the main
social center. Much of town life focused around these

Taverns were popular gathering spots
during colonial times. They served as
meetinghouses, and restaurants.

places. People from all classes of society enjoyed spending time in taverns.

When an important ship pulled into the harbor
and dropped anchor, a crew member would fire a gun
to let the people know the latest news had arrived. The
ship's captain would take the letters he had carried
across the ocean to the tavern or coffee house to distrib-
ute them.

If a town couldn't afford a tavern, a farmer might be given money to put an "ordinary" in his home, where he would provide a traveler with food, a bed, and feed for his horses.

A farmer who ran an "ordinary" could expect to earn a slightly better living than his neighbors.

As urban cities grew, taverns became very important to the population. There were many different kinds of taverns. Some were very elegant, others very plain and rough. Taverns served as meetinghouses, market places, restaurants, political arenas, and dance halls.

The townsfolk came to eat, drink, post notices on the walls for all to read, discuss acts of parliament, and exchange ideas on religion and politics. Men gathered in taverns to talk about the heavy taxes and unfair "acts" imposed on the colonies by the English king. These discussions led to the decision to join together to put an end to English rule. Some taverns and inns became famous meeting places for the Sons of Liberty during the struggle for independence.

Entertainment was an important part of tavern life. A wide variety of diversions such as games, singing, and dancing took place there. Although laws existed to prevent most of these festive activities, they were generally ignored.

Taverns in the south were usually less successful than those in the north because the communities there were not so centralized. Taverns outside of cities never really became important social centers. In wilderness areas, the fort became the center of social activity.

Women were most often excluded from tavern life, except to go to dinner or maybe a dance or another public function. Women did, however, operate some of the taverns. This usually happened after a woman's husband had died and she took over as the proprietor.

Servants, apprentices, black settlers, and seamen

weren't allowed in a tavern without permission from their master or captain. Even though there were laws against serving African Americans, records indicate that many of them used taverns as much as other people. There were also ordinances against serving liquor to Native Americans, but many tavern owners disregarded the law.

Large urban taverns required plenty of help. They used servants, freed blacks, white indentured servants, and slaves to fill the need. It often took as many slaves to run a large tavern as it did to maintain a plantation household.

Coffee houses were more specialized than other types of taverns. Their activities centered around the business community. Mercantile exchanges and auctions took place there.

For many of the men of colonial times, joining a social club was considered the perfect form of recreation. These social clubs met at taverns. The men got together to play cards and billiards, have a few drinks, eat a meal, and talk about conditions within the colonies. Some of the earliest clubs were formed by the French, Irish, and Italian settlers. There were also other fraternal orders and societies that met during the early days of America.

CHAPTER SEVEN

Entertainment and Pastimes

T he settlers participated in a variety of activities for amusement. They found relief from their daily tasks by either seeking out a soothing pastime or taking part in a more stimulating form of entertainment.

SIMPLE PLEASURES

Most early Americans worked very hard, and when they had a chance to relax, they enjoyed life's simplest pleasures. Children liked to daydream while swinging on a gate or relaxing in a large stack of hay. Feeding the farm animals, picking berries, or getting pushed around the farm in a wheelbarrow also provided many happy moments for colonial boys and girls.

Children were expected to learn helpful skills early in life. Youngsters took pride in their accomplishments. Girls learned to sew by the age of five; they were able to knit, weave, embroider, and do needlework. It was customary for a young girl to stitch a sampler with a lovely picture or Bible verse on it. Her handiwork was then proudly displayed in the home.

Young Native American girls were taught the skills that were considered necessary. They could weave mats and baskets and make their own clothes.

Both boys and girls learned to whittle—forming objects out of wood by cutting or paring—and a colonial girl could whittle as well as any boy. The children made things like birch brooms with their knives. Trading and barter were very common. Children could get items they wanted by trading. Girls often exchanged their handmade things for laces and ribbons. Boys usually looked for small gadgets and toys in return for their work.

Reading was a popular activity for many colonists. Many people liked to read from books of poetry, and some talented settlers wrote poems of their own. Many families could recite from the Bible or the works of Shakespeare.

The first book of original poems published in America was in the year 1650 by Anne Bradstreet. Anne was a Puritan who lived in the Massachusetts Bay Colony. Phillis Wheatley, a poet, was the first African-American woman to have her work published in the United States.

Benjamin Franklin started the first circulating library in the colonies in Philadelphia in 1731. In 1732, his first almanac was published. He wrote almanacs for over twenty years. These works became known as *Poor Richard's Almanack* because Ben Franklin wrote them under the pen name of Richard Saunders. Many of his famous sayings such as *"Early to bed and early to rise, makes a man healthy, wealthy, and wise"* were first printed in these almanacs.

FAMILY PASTIMES

Colonial families were very close, and the home was the center of most of their activity. Many evenings were spent with the children, parents, and grandparents gathered around the fireplace. It was common to find a seat built in on each side of a colonial fireplace. The boys and girls liked to curl into these seats, listen to the family chatter, and watch the sparks from the fire soar upward.

Grandparents contributed much to the family's entertainment, and the children often discovered that these family elders were filled with ideas, stories, and knowledge of their ancestral history. It was often a grandparent who kept the family entranced around the fire for an evening of storytelling.

Families enjoyed telling their favorite stories over and over again. Many of them were folktales that had come from their homeland and had been heard by many generations. These tales were frequently used as a way to pass along the family's history.

Certain groups of people like the Amish and Old Order Mennonites in the Pennsylvania colony didn't keep church records. They preferred to pass on their religious beliefs and folk customs orally.

Among African Americans, their traditional folktales were one of the cultural customs to survive in the colonies. Within the slaves' quarters, folktales and songs were an important and distinctive cultural form. Their stories had been passed down from the lore of tribes like the Ewe, Ashanti, and Ibo.

Many of the children of slaves learned of the customs and languages of Africa through these tales. The African folktales, much like the European ones, were often about an animal that had the power of speech and was wise and clever. The animal always triumphed

The home was the center of most activities
for the colonists. Many evenings were
spent gathered around the fireplace.

over evil. Some common animals in these folktales were
the rabbit, spider, or the Nigerian tortoise. Through
their folklore, it was easy to see that the Africans valued
their families, children, and knowledge.

For thousands of years Native Americans had been
passing down their people's beliefs through vivid stories told by their tribal elders. This is how their younger
generation learned of their tribe's history and beliefs.
"Singing birds" is what many Native Americans called

their storytellers. Some northeastern groups gathered in their longhouses to tell their tales. Other tribes sat around bonfires to listen to their storytellers. Clans often retold the tale of how their people came to be.

During the warm spring and summer months, when a family could pursue an outdoor activity, the garden was a great source of joy. This was especially true for the colonial wife who could find comfort in recreating a garden scene similar to the one she had enjoyed in her homeland.

Gardens were both useful and lovely. People grew vegetables for food, and they planted flowers and shrubs to add beauty, color, and fragrance around their homes.

Herb gardens were grown near the kitchen where it was handy for the housewife to gather plants she needed to make a tasty meal or herbs for medicine when one of the family was ill. Colonial housewives collected sage, parsley, thyme, basil, and oregano plus many other plants for use in their homes. Sweet-smelling herbs came in handy in making gifts such as sachets. Herbs were not the only plants used for flavorings by colonial cooks—marigold petals and rose petals were also popular seasonings.

Gardens were carefully planned and faithfully tended. The colonists took great pride in their handiwork. It was fashionable to escort visitors out to the family garden to show it off. Most gardens were divided in half with a walkway down the center. Some families placed benches in the area so they could sit outside when the weather allowed.

Slaves worked in their small family gardens on Sunday afternoons. These gardens helped supply their families with extra food.

During the colonial era, there were not many opportunities for women to own and operate a small business. Women were expected to stay at home and take care of their husbands and families. Men ran most of the shops in the town except for a few jobs that were considered women's work. Some women, however, were able to have a business dealing in flower and vegetable seeds.

LIVELY ENTERTAINMENT

People of early America loved music, singing, and dancing. These diversions were prohibited in certain areas for religious reasons, but people found ways to enjoy these amusements despite the restrictions. Adults, children, slaves, servants, masters, and Native Americans all incorporated the world of music into their lives.

Dances ranged from very elegant balls that had been planned for weeks or months to casual, good time get-togethers arranged on the spur of the moment.

Plantation owners were known for the formal balls they held, but it wasn't unusual for people to burst into an unplanned dance session when the mood struck them. For a fancy ball, neighboring families and often dignitaries were invited to the plantation. An elaborate well-planned banquet would be laid out on a table, and people feasted and danced beneath candlelit chandeliers all night.

In the Middle and New England colonies, the long floor plan of a tavern made it an excellent place to hold a dance. There were three types of dances held in a tavern. They were private parties that people attended by invitation only, public balls that citizens were permitted to attend by purchasing a ticket, and dancing assemblies that were open to the public.

Some colonists didn't think it proper for men and women to dance together. They preferred formal, dig-

A dress ball was one form
of entertainment reserved for
wealthy plantation owners.

nified assemblies. Some popular colonial dances were minuets, jigs, reels, marches, hornpipes, and square dances. The Virginia reel became well known and was often an important event of the evening during a plantation ball.

Town dances were more formal than country dances. When people gathered for a country spree, everyone from the youngest to the oldest showed up. The country folk had fun square dancing, then called country dancing, and filling up on a buffet dinner. The dancing often lasted all night.

This activity became so popular that dancing schools soon appeared in the colonies. Children of wealthy families, and boys and girls who lived on plantations, received their dance lessons from an instructor who lived with their family.

On a plantation, music for an event might be provided by slaves playing fiddles and banjos. They were often expert musicians. If the plantation owners were throwing an elegant ball, they usually had several talented players to supply the evening's musical entertainment.

A colonial fiddler had many places to perform his craft. He provided music for formal and informal dances, and at country fairs, cornhuskings, and barn raisings as well.

In some places, people belonged to a choir or played in a quartet as a popular diversion. This was especially true in the Middle colonies.

Some of the instruments that were popular at the time were: spinet, harpsichord, pianoforte, viol, violin, guitar, German flute, drum, fife, French horn, Jew's harp, violoncello, fiddle, flute, trumpet, and trombone. Nothing could stop the settlers from making their music. If there were no instruments, they made their own with paper-covered combs, spoons, tin kettles, pokers, or tongs. They knew how to turn almost any gadget into a musical instrument.

Many families considered it important for their children to learn to play an instrument. If the family could afford to hire a live-in teacher, boys and girls were taught at home.

Boys were taught to play the drum, fife, or horn, while girls learned to master the harpsichord or spinet.

Slaves in colonial America
depended on music to help
brighten their lives.

African Americans depended on music to brighten
their lives, and despite all the restrictions placed upon
them, the slaves were able to draw from their heritage
to build a strong musical tradition that has continued to
this day.

Some of the slaves' favorite instruments were the

banjo, fiddle, and drum. They made a drum by hollowing out a piece of wood and stretching an animal skin over it. They also played the clarinet, fife, tambourine, triangle, flute, and a three-stringed instrument similar to a banjo.

Singing helped relieve the burden of working all day, every day. Slaves toiling in the fields sang songs of sorrow and hope.

The slaves also adapted Christian hymns to their unique blend of African rhythms and created the black spirituals. There was a distinct feature to African music and rhythmic complexity that was superior to the European music. Europeans based their music on one rhythm only, while an African tune sometimes had three rhythmic patterns or more.

Dancing was important to the slaves. African dance involved rapid movements where the dancers leaped to the beat of a drum. It was an excellent way to relieve stress and enliven dismal days. It wasn't unusual for the slaves to organize a dance party without the master's permission. All nearby slaves were invited to these gatherings.

The slaves sometimes performed their tribal songs and dances to entertain the plantation family or for the amusement of their fellow slaves.

Music and dance had always been an important part of Native American culture. Native Americans created their instruments from natural materials, rather than from metals as the colonists did. They made reed flutes, wooden drums, and gourd rattles. These instruments played a significant role in their ceremonies and in their lives. Gourd rattles were used during religious rituals, and in warfare, the beat of the drum carried a special meaning.

Native Americans held dances for many reasons. If they wanted to call attention to the gods during a dry spell, they did a rain dance. They did a victory dance after winning a war and upon returning from a successful expedition. They painted their faces before a dance and wore animal skins on their wrists and quivers of arrows and clubs on their backs while carrying bows in their hands. It was customary for Indians to dance in a circle while stamping their feet and shouting.

If the colonists weren't attending a dance, they could find other pleasing diversions such as spending an evening at the theater. The first theatrical show performed in the colonies was *The Bear and The Cub* in 1665 in the Virginia colony.

Drama took place in a tavern, a courtroom, or a warehouse so that a large number of people could attend. These "theaters" often accommodated as many as three hundred people. The first colonial theaters appeared in the bigger, more important taverns in towns like Williamsburg, Virginia; New York City, New York; Charleston, South Carolina; and Philadelphia, Pennsylvania. Shakespeare's *King Lear* and *Romeo and Juliet* were popular plays during this time.

Early theaters were unheated. It was a common practice for a woman to send her servant to the theater at about four in the afternoon to reserve a good seat and keep it warm for her.

Occasionally, colonial families could catch a puppet or horse show in town. The Punch and Judy puppet show was popular during the early days of our nation. The circus and menagerie were beginning to form at this time, giving people the rare opportunity to see exotic animals. There were also exhibits that displayed gadgets and new inventions.

CHAPTER EIGHT

Early American Observances

The people of early America believed that certain events called for the joining of family, friends, and neighbors to share memories or to assemble for a good time.

FESTIVE DAYS

Any reason to rejoice and be merry made life more fulfilling for the settlers. The birth of a baby was cause for celebration. Family members would gather to welcome the new addition. Some settlers announced the arrival of their new child by tying a ribbon to the front door—blue for a boy and white for a girl.

For many Christian families, a baby's baptism brought the kinfolk together for a party. The Dutch settlers had the custom of giving an "apostle spoon" to a child on the day of christening. Molded at the end of the handle was the figure of the saint or apostle for whom the newborn had been named. The infant's name and the date were also engraved on the spoon. This gift was most often given by the baby's godparents.

Colonial girls and boys looked forward to their birthdays. During the very early settlement years, most birthdays went unnoticed. As time went on, however, remembering a child's day of birth was considered a special event by the family. On this day, some youngsters were permitted to skip their usual chores. They took advantage of the free time to enjoy themselves.

Fortunate children had birthday parties where sweet treats, pastries, fruit, cheese, and tea were served. Boys and girls received practical gifts as birthday presents.

A hope chest was the usual gift for a young woman soon to be married. Over the years, she would fill this trunk, sometimes referred to as "the home of her hopes," with items to use upon her marriage. For birthdays, and other special occasions, a young woman would be given things such as linen and needlework to add to her hope chest. A lucky bride had a full trunk when she married.

Some colonists acknowledged the birthdays of England's royal family. On these occasions, people would fire guns or set off fireworks.

A wedding in the colonial period was an event eagerly awaited. Many marriages took place during the Christmas season. Settlers were too busy at harvest time to leave their work and attend a party. The Dutch colonists preferred Pinkster Dagh in the spring as the beginning of their wedding season.

A wedding could take place in the church or at home. Southern marriages commonly took place in the home where family and friends joined the couple to share a huge banquet.

A magistrate performed the marriage ceremony in the New England colonies. The Puritans considered

The birth of a child, baptisms, feast days,
birthdays—all were cause for a good time.
This is a picture of a Pilgrim wedding.

marriage more of a public contract than a religious
ritual.

The Dutch settlers presented a "monkey spoon" to
the happy newlyweds. This spoon had the symbol of a
monkey drinking from a goblet, which represented fes-

tivity. The spoon often carried a heart on the handle, and under the figure of the monkey there was a picture of a bridal couple and the names and the date engraved on it as a special remembrance.

Most colonial weddings took place in the afternoon and the celebrating lasted more than one day. Many families had unique traditions that they observed on these occasions.

The night before a wedding, a dance was commonly held at the house of the bride. The following morning, the bridal procession lined up at her home. After the couple had dressed in their wedding clothes, they drove to the church in a horse-drawn carriage followed by all of their guests. The horses were decorated with colored ribbons. In the winter, a sleigh carried the joyous couple to the church and the brisk air that surrounded them was filled with the sounds of carols as the crowd sang.

After the ceremony, people had fun racing each other back to the bride's house. No one passed the bridal party, however, because this was regarded as very bad manners. Upon returning to the bride's home, the guests filled up on the tasty dinner that was offered. The Sunday following the marriage, after everyone had rested, was a special day in honor of the new bride and groom. This day was marked with more singing, dancing, and eating.

Wedding cakes were often baked with a piece of nutmeg tucked inside. The settlers believed that whoever received the portion of cake with the spice in it would be the next to marry.

Indentured servants weren't permitted to marry during their service. If one of these young men or women fell in love, they had to put off their wedding plans until they were free. This often meant waiting a long time.

For America's original inhabitants, marriage meant

the union of two clans. Some Native American tribes held a two-part wedding ceremony. The first was a private event that occurred between the young couple and their kinfolk when the families exchanged gifts. The second part of the ritual involved the whole village. Everyone gathered for a huge feast in honor of the couple and their marriage.

Some colonists commemorated the feast day of their favorite saint. The Dutch honored St. Martin's Day each fall with a banquet. They made a special dish containing beef and vegetables called "hodge podge," or "hutspot" on this day. For these settlers, it was a time of thanksgiving. Many of the people celebrated St. Martin's Eve like Halloween. They believed ghosts and goblins inhabited the earth on this night.

St. George's Day was remembered in Williamsburg with a fair in the market square, and St. Tammany's Day was observed in Philadelphia with music and feasting. St. Steven's Day, the day after Christmas, was a special occasion for the early English settlers, while the French honored St. Catherine's Day.

In March, maple season brought along happy times for many pioneers. The Dutch men would bore holes in the maple trees once the sap started running. A hollow tube was inserted into the hole so that the sap dripped into a bucket. The Dutch had learned the art of tapping trees from the Indians. The sap was gathered from many buckets and then emptied into huge kettles that had been suspended over wood fires. It was then boiled until it thickened into a syrup, or longer until it turned into sugar.

The women and children liked to join the men in the woods for a maple festival. They would have a party with games and singing. The children loved to make taffy by pouring hot syrup over cold snow.

The Iroquois Indians had been celebrating the maple harvest for thousands of years. They poured maple syrup over popcorn, calling the treat "snow food," and over other foods such as cakes and cornmeal. They also made maple sugar candy. Mixing the syrup with strawberries, blueberries, or other kinds of berries to make a delicious fruit drink was also popular with Native Americans.

COLONIAL FUNERALS

A funeral was an important social event for colonial families. It brought together relatives and neighbors. During the early days, people were more concerned with displaying their wealth at the funeral of a loved one than showing their grief. Among some settlers, more festivities occurred during a funeral than at a wedding.

Wealthy families thought it appropriate to pass out little gifts such as scarves, gloves, or rings to all who attended.

In New England, children were also included at these social functions where people gathered for much feasting and drinking.

Funerals were eventually banned on Sundays in the city of Boston because large crowds, including servants and children, followed the coffin through the streets. The authorities considered such a commotion on the sacred day improper. After all, Sunday was supposed to be a somber, respectful day.

It was common practice for a boy or girl to be a pallbearer at the funeral of a friend. Young unmarried men and women were also responsible for carrying the coffin of one of their friends. There were no undertakers in colonial times. The body of the deceased had to be cared for by the family, friends, or someone from the church. A member of the church was often paid to take invitations around the town. No one dared show up who had not been invited. The Dutch colonists served *doed-koecks*, or dead cakes, that displayed the name of the deceased and the date. These were mementos and could be saved for years. They also made *rouw koeken*, or mourning cakes, that were served with wine.

"Monkey spoons" were also given at funerals as reminders of the event. The bowl of the spoon showed a single figure of the "inviter" greeting the guests. The name of the person who had died and the date would be inscribed on the handle.

Since there were no funeral homes in those days, the dead person had to be "laid out" at home. The family most often chose the best room in the house for this purpose. If they were well-to-do, a family usually had a room just for this purpose. The Dutch called this room the *doed-dramer*.

Dutch women didn't follow the body to the grave. They stayed at home and ate little cakes, drank spiced wine, and gossiped. When the men returned from the grave site, they found that the women had prepared the table with food, pipes, and tobacco. The men then ate, drank, and smoked long into the night.

Funerals were especially important to African Americans. Many people recalled the expensive, long, drawn-out affairs that had taken place in their native land. They believed in a long period of mourning and the burial of personal objects with the body. Africans believed that when a person died, he or she went "home."

For the slaves who lived on the plantations, burials and ceremonies had to take place at night because the people weren't allowed to stop working during the day to bury the dead. It was often weeks after the death before people could gather and celebrate the journey home of the one they had lost.

AMERICAN INDIAN CEREMONIES

Native American ceremonies often centered around life-giving substances such as food, rain, and sun. Native Americans had a deep respect for nature and believed in giving thanks. They also held rituals to mark important events.

Each Native American group had special beliefs and celebrations, but many ceremonies were shared by the different tribes. The Iroquois Indians held six ceremonies of thanksgiving each year.

These occasions were marked with feelings of hope and gratitude. Native Americans performed songs and dances at these events. Many people still practice these rituals. They believe they have a responsibility to carry on these sacred traditions.

The Iroquois tribes began their ceremonial year with the Mid-Winter Festival. This took place in January or February and lasted about nine days.

Next, they celebrated Thanks-to-the Maple in late March. The people left the village at this time to camp near family-owned maple groves. They spent several weeks in the woods and returned to their villages before the spring thaw.

The Corn Planting Festival occurred in May or June when the time was right to plant the corn.

The Strawberry Festival in June was their next celebration. Small groups of women and children and sometimes men made picnic parties and went into the hills to gather strawberries.

The Green Corn Ceremony took place in August or September when the corn was ready for picking. It lasted four days. This celebration marked the middle of their year. Choosing names for the tribe's infants occurred twice a year, once at the Mid-Winter Festival and again at the Green Corn Ceremony. All children

Native Americans held ceremonies
and celebrations to honor nature.
They gave thanks to the gods for
such things as their food, the rain,
and the sun. This is a depiction of the
green corn dance, performed
when the corn was ready for harvest.

who had been born since the ritual in the winter were
given names during this ceremony.

And last, Native Americans held the Harvest Festival. This took place in October when the people offered thanks for their food.

Southern Native American tribes observed the Huskanaw—a ceremony to initiate boys into manhood. This was a special test to see if the boys were ready to become men, and to learn if any talented young men were ready to become leaders of their tribe.

The Huskanaw Ceremony began with a two-day dance in the woods involving the whole tribe. People would form two large circles, one circle went clockwise and the other counterclockwise.

The boys in the Native American tribes of the northeast became men when they took on a guardian spirit through a vision or a dream rather than a Huskanaw.

CHAPTER NINE

Working Bees

E stablishing a new territory required lots of hard work. The land had to be cleared so that homes, schools, churches, and shops could be built. Food had to be planted, harvested, and stored for the winter. By working together, people accomplished their tasks in less time and with much less difficulty than by doing the job alone.

The pioneers knew the importance of uniting to complete a task. Early settlers were neighborly and willing to pitch in and help one another. Holding a "bee" was their special way of combining work with pleasure.

These working parties brought pleasure into the lives of farm families who were happy to get away from their isolation and visit with neighbors. For the Puritans, a working bee provided the rare chance for a good time and the opportunity for the young men and women of the village to meet and get to know each other.

When the work was finished, the fun began. People gathered together for food, games, contests, and entertainment. Eating was an important part of a bee and each family contributed to the meal. Entertainment was frequently furnished by a local fiddler, and the settlers danced and sang while he played.

Holding contests amused many people. To prove strength, men wrestled one another. They also found it a challenge to see who could jump the highest or longest distance. Wrestling a bear cub was also thought of as a manly feat. A few bold men would snatch a scattering of ants off a maple tree stump and gobble them down or eat as many raw eggs as possible in order to show off. Some men gulped thirty or forty eggs at one sitting.

Any chore, big or small, could be completed at a working bee. While the men labored, the women prepared the food for the delicious buffet that followed the finished job.

Working side by side, early settlers filled their new land with homes, roads, and bridges that benefited everyone.

GET THE JOB DONE

A "raising day" was one of the most festive occasions for the settlers. People joined forces when a home, barn, or schoolhouse needed to be built. Everyone in the community offered strong arms, sturdy backs, and their skills to help out.

It was a pleasing sight for a newcomer to an area to see fellow settlers arriving to assist. It was also common for the people to help out a newly married couple or a neighbor who had had a run of bad luck.

Before a building could be constructed, the land had to be cleared. The townsfolk arrived prepared for the job, leading their powerful teams of oxen and carrying their sharp axes. They held chopping bees, log-

The colonists banded together to help one another when land needed to be cleared and homes built. These working parties combined hard work and great fun.

ging bees, and stump-pulling bees to prepare the land for homes and other buildings.

If a large area of land needed to be cleared, the men formed teams and competed to see who was the fastest. A jug of whiskey was often given as a prize to the winning team.

The settlers chose to clear the land in the spring. The wood was then left to dry during the hot summer months and when fall arrived, the pioneers set the treetops and smaller branches on fire. The large trunks of the trees were collected into stacks during a piling bee, and all the leftover debris was pushed into piles and burned again.

In the rocky New England area, stones had to be hauled away before homes could be built or fields planted. Stone bees were held to clear away the stones.

Once autumn arrived, the settlers kept busy harvesting and preserving their food for the long winter ahead. Apple bees took place at this time. People had to core and pare the apples in order to prepare them for the winter. They made treats like cider and applesauce from the juicy fruit.

Husking bees were enjoyed by the young and old alike. Huge stacks of corn were dumped onto the barn floor. The whole community pitched in to help turn the dull job of husking all that corn into a festive event.

Corn was an important part of the early American diet. Many families survived almost completely on food made from corn, such as corn mush, corn gruel, corn dumplings, corn cakes, and corn on the cob for a good part of the year.

With the exhausting work of harvest almost finished, the husking bee was looked forward to as a time for good fellowship and fun, and as the social event of October. Usually, the people divided into two teams and raced against one another to see which team finished shucking their stack of corn first. The waiting bins filled quickly as the members of each team tore the outer leaves off of the corncobs as rapidly as possible and tossed them in.

Men and women sat in alternate seats while working, and when a man found a red ear of corn, he was permitted to kiss the woman sitting next to him. Another common practice was to declare the person who peeled the last ear of corn the winner.

The husking bee gave the slaves in the south a chance for a little fun and socializing. After the corn had been picked and stacked in the barn, all the slaves in the area were brought together to join in the shucking. Plenty of talking, joking, laughing, and singing took place.

In the late fall, usually in November, families started their butchering. This was especially true for the German settlers in the Pennsylvania colony.

Neighbors gathered at the host farm before the first light of morning. The beef, cattle, and hogs had already been butchered so that the work could begin. The people held bees for cutting the meat, making sausage and scrapple, rendering the lard, and smoking the hams and bacon over a fire of green hickory chips.

Late at night, after sharing rye whiskey, the neighbors returned home. They left carrying a supply of sausage and fresh meat to show for their hard day's work.

Native American women also joined with one another for working bees. The women did most of the planting and preparing of the food for their families and clans. The women united in female parties to till the ground, gather the firewood, and pound the corn in mortars.

SPECIAL TALENTS

Women within the community, whether they were old, young, married or single, were all welcome at the quilt-

Quilting bees brought women together
to stitch beautiful quilts and socialize.

ing bee. One neighbor at a time would host the bee in
her home. The women arrived carrying heaps of rags
to add to the quilt. Every scrap of fabric was put to use.
Neighbors frequently traded squares of material to
obtain a greater variety. The star, as well as an eagle, a
basket of flowers, or a piece of fruit, were all popular
designs of the time and were stitched into the quilt
patterns.

The Pennsylvania Dutch were quite skilled in crafts, and when these women set out to create a beautiful quilt, their talents were displayed. They were known for arranging their colorful squares into a lovely patchwork pattern.

Knitting bees were also useful events. Women of the town came together to share their skills and create many beautiful items.

A young woman liked to work on a quilt or collect other homemade items that could be used to fill her hope chest.

In the early evening, after the women had finished with their sewing, the men arrived to share dinner and tea. Biscuits, tarts, and cake preserves were served.

More than a few of the settlers liked to demonstrate their singing abilities at a singing bee. The people not only competed to see who had the best voice but spent time listening to music and dancing.

Spelling bees were usually held to challenge the youngsters. Boys and girls hoped they could recall their lessons as they attempted to spell long and difficult words. Proud was the child who could outdo the others.

From time to time, men and women got together for a custom called changework. Two people who had the same job to accomplish worked with one another. If two of the neighborhood women needed to complete a task such as making soap or putting together a rag carpet, they would do it together. The women worked at one of their homes for a few days, and then they switched and did the chore at the other home.

Taste of dinner was a pleasant New England custom. A family would send small portions or just a "taste" of goodies to tempt a tired neighbor or a lonely friend into joining them for dinner. It was also customary to send a bountiful supply of food as a gift for a wedding reception or other social occasion.

A GOOD TIME

Despite all of the work that constantly awaited the settlers, from time to time, they came together just for the fun of it.

In November, when the French settlers were honoring St. Catherine, they held taffy-pulling bees. This started their season of romance. These bees brought together the young men and women of the village for fun and to sample the treat. The young people boiled molasses into a syrup, and after it cooled and formed a sticky taffy, they rolled it into long strips.

Sparking bees were joyous assemblies held so that the young women and men of the community could get to know each other. If a couple's interest was sparked while at the bee, and a courtship developed, the community would soon be dancing at their wedding.

Whether the settlers held a bee to accomplish a difficult task or just to have a good time, the results were the same. People were there for one another through the good times and the bad.

America was built by the creative talents of all its people. Settlers from many countries and varied cultures, Native Americans who had been surviving as one with the land for thousands of years, African slaves who were forced to live in the colonies, and indentured servants who were obliged to serve their masters, all had a hand in forming the present American culture. Our holiday customs, leisure-time activities, favorite sports, and well-loved recreations come from all Americans.

Games–Goodies–Gifts

WORD GAME: *INTRY, MINTRY*

Intry, mintry, cutry, corn,
Briar seeds and apple thorns,
Briars, wire, limber lock,
Five geese in a flock,
Sit and sing,
By the spring,
O-u-t and in again.

OUTDOOR TAG GAME: *FOX AND GEESE*

This tag game is easily played in the snow where the players can mark out a large wagon wheel. The wheel's outer circle should be approximately fifty feet in diameter. There should be eight spokes across it and a small circle in the center. The small circle is home base for the players called geese. The players run around the spokes and rim, while the person who is "it" (the fox) tries to

99

tag them. When geese are caught, they must help tag the others.

GAME WITH TOP: *CHIPSTONES*

Players mark off a five-foot circle. Each player then places a small, flat stone inside the circle and takes a turn launching a top into the circle. As the top is spinning, the player slides a small plank or shovel beneath it and carries the moving top to a stone. He drops the spinning top so that it hits the chipstone's edge and flips the stone out of the circle. A player is permitted to keep trying as long as his top remains spinning. A player may start his top and take another turn if he has flipped a stone out of the ring. The winner is the player who has moved the most stones.

MAPLE TREAT: *SUGAR-ON-SNOW*

Ingredients: Pure Maple Syrup
   Bring to a boil one quart of maple syrup. Cook until the temperature reaches 232°–236°F., or when a small spoonful of syrup will stay on the surface of firmly packed snow. After cooling, you should be able to lift it easily with a fork. Simply wind it onto the fork and enjoy. Some people prefer to make puddles, others "string" the syrup out on the snow. One quart serves about six to eight people.
(Courtesy of George L. Cook, UVM Extension Maple Agent Morrisville, Vermont)

PILGRIM FAVORITE: *FURMENTY*

Ingredients: 1 cup cracked wheat, 1 quart water, 3/4 cup milk, 1/2 cup heavy cream, 1/2 tsp. salt, 1/8 tsp.

ground mace, 1/2 tsp. ground cinnamon, 1/4 cup brown sugar, 2 egg yolks, and additional brown sugar. In a large pot, bring the water to a boil and add the wheat. Lower heat to simmer, cover, and continue to cook for a half hour, or until soft. Drain off all the water and add the milk, cream, salt, mace, cinnamon, and sugar. Continue to simmer, stirring occasionally, until most of the liquid is absorbed (20 to 30 minutes). In a small bowl, beat the egg yolks and slowly stir 1/2 cup of the wheat mixture into the yolks. Then add the yolk mixture to the pot, stir, and continue cooking for another five minutes, stirring frequently. Serve sprinkled with brown sugar. Serves eight to ten people.
(Courtesy of the Plimoth Plantation)

DUTCH CHRISTMAS COOKIES: *SPECULAAS*

Ingredients: 1 cup butter, 1 cup brown sugar, 1 cup white sugar, 2 eggs, 4 cups flour, 1 tsp. baking soda, 1-1/2 tsps. cinnamon, 3/4 tsp. ground ginger, 3/4 tsp. ground cloves, 3/4 tsp. ground allspice, approximately 1/4 cup milk, and 1/2 cup nuts, chopped fine.

In a large bowl, cream the butter and sugars. Beat in eggs, one at a time. Sift flour, baking soda, and spices. Stir to blend; then knead gently. Add milk as needed to make a smooth dough. Add nuts and chill in refrigerator about two hours. Roll out dough on floured board until it is 1/8-inch thick, and cut into fancy Christmas shapes. Bake in preheated oven, 350°, for ten minutes. Makes eight dozen cookies.
(Courtesy of the Historical Society of Rockland County, New York)

TASTY BERRY DRINK: *RASPBERRY FLUMMERY*

Ingredients: 2 cups raspberries (or berry of your choice), 1/2 cup cold water, 1 cup sugar, 1/2 tsp. salt, and 4 Tbs. cornstarch.

Wash the berries. Remove stems and leaves. Place berries in a two-quart saucepan with 1/2 cup cold water. Cover and cook over medium heat until the berries are soft, approximately ten minutes.

Mix the sugar, salt, and cornstarch in a small bowl. Slowly add this to the berries, stirring. Turn the heat to low and cook, while stirring, until the mixture thickens, about five minutes.

Spoon the flummery into fancy glasses and chill in the refrigerator. Makes four servings.

FRAGRANT GIFT: *POMANDER BALL*

Materials: a soft-skinned, medium-sized orange (or lemon), a box of cloves about 1-3/4 ounces, satin ribbon 1/2-inch wide in the color of your choice, a thin nail, and a piece of string.

Make a tiny hole in the skin of the fruit with the nail and place a clove in the hole. Repeat the process until the surface of the orange is well covered, with enough of the skin showing to separate the cloves.

Temporarily tie the string around the orange from bottom to top on four sides with a loop at the top. Hang the pomander ball in a cool, dry place until the surface begins to dry and the orange has started to shrink a little.

Remove the string, and add a colored ribbon tied in the same manner as the string, with the loop at the top as long as needed to hang the pomander ball.

Glossary

Ancestral—having to do with an ancestor or ancestors

Anthropologist—one who studies the origins of man, including the social, physical, behavioral, and cultural development

Apprentice—a person who is under agreement to work for another in order to learn a trade

Continental Congress—before the Revolutionary War, this was an advisory council consisting of delegates from the American colonies; it later became the central government of the United States

General Court—a colonial legislative body with judicial power

Indentured servant—a person bound by a contract to another for a specific amount of time, usually four to seven years, to pay off passage to the colonies; a servant to a master

Longhouse—a long communal dwelling especially of the Iroquois

Magistrate—a civil officer with the power to administer and enforce laws; a justice of the peace

Matzohs—unleavened bread, made without yeast so that it does not rise

Muster—assemble troops for roll call, review, exercise, inspection, and service

Pomander—a mixture of aromatic substances often in the form of a ball

Sachet—a small fragrant packet used to scent clothes stored in trunks or closets

Sampler—a decorative piece of needlework typically having letters or verses embroidered on it in various stitches as an example of skill

Scrapple—a mush of pork scraps and cornmeal; after it sets, the scrapple is sliced and fried

Shaman—a priest or medicine man among certain North American Native Americans

Sons of Liberty—a secret revolutionary society

Switch—a thin flexible twig, rod, or stick

Bibliography

Anderson, Joan. *The First Thanksgiving Feast.* 2nd ed. New York: Houghton Mifflin, 1990.

Back to Basics. How to Learn and Enjoy Traditional American Skills. Pleasantville, NY: Reader's Digest Assoc., Inc., 1981.

Borreson, Mary Jo. *Let's Go To Colonial Williamsburg.* New York: G.P. Putnam's Sons, 1961.

Brown, Ira L. *The Georgia Colony.* A Forge of Freedom Book. New York: Crowell-Collier Press, 1970.

Costabel, Eva Deutsch. *The Jews of New Amsterdam.* New York: Atheneum Macmillan, 1988.

_____. *The Pennsylvania Dutch: Craftsmen and Farmers.* New York: Atheneum Macmillan, 1986.

Fradin, Dennis B. *Delaware in Pictures and Words.* Chicago: Childrens Press, 1980.

_____. *The New York Colony.* Chicago: Childrens Press, 1988.

_____. *The Virginia Colony.* Chicago: Childrens Press, 1986.

Glubok, Shirley, ed. *Home and Child Life in Colonial Days.* New York: Macmillan, 1969.

Hawke, David Freeman. *Everyday Life in Early America.* New York: Harper and Row, 1988.

Kalman, Bobbie. *Early Christmas.* The Early Settlers Series. New York: Crabtree Publishing Co., 1981.

———. *Early Pleasures and Pastimes.* The Early Settlers Series. New York: Crabtree Publishing Co., 1983.

———. *Early Village Life.* The Early Settlers Series. New York: Crabtree Publishing Co., 1981.

Rice, Kym S. *Early American Taverns: For the Entertainment of Friends and Strangers.* Chicago: Regnery Gateway, 1983.

Smith, Robert. *The Massachusetts Colony.* A Forge of Freedom Book. New York: Crowell-Collier Press, 1969.

Spier, Peter. *The Legend of New Amsterdam.* Garden City, NY: Doubleday and Co., 1979.

Stevens, S.K. *The Pennsylvania Colony.* A Forge of Freedom Book. New York: Crowell-Collier Press, 1970.

The Story of America. A National Geographic Picture Atlas. Washington, D.C.: National Geographic Society, 1984.

For Further Reading

Anderson, Joan. *The First Thanksgiving Feast*. 2nd ed. New York: Houghton Mifflin, 1990.

Borreson, Mary Jo. *Let's Go To Colonial Williamsburg*. New York: G.P. Putnam's Sons, 1961.

Costabel, Eva Deutsch. *The Jews of New Amsterdam*. New York: Atheneum Macmillan, 1988.

Glubok, Shirley, ed. *Home and Child Life in Colonial Days*. New York: Macmillan, 1969.

Kalman, Bobbie. *Early Christmas*. The Early Settlers Series. New York: Crabtree Publishing Co., 1981.

_____. *Early Pleasures and Pastimes*. The Early Settlers Series. New York: Crabtree Publishing Co., 1983.

Spier, Peter. *The Legend of New Amsterdam*. Garden City, NY: Doubleday and Co., 1979.

Index

About the Author

Karen Helene Lizon lives in rural central New York with her husband and their three children—Luke, Autumn, and Anthony. This is her first book for children.